How to play the Penny Whistle

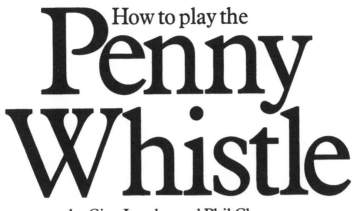

by Gina Landor and Phil Cleaver

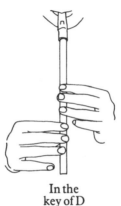

In the
key of D

ISBN: 978-0-8600-1780-6

HAL•LEONARD®

Visit Hal Leonard Online at
www.halleonard.com

World headquarters, contact:
Hal Leonard
7777 West Bluemound Road
Milwaukee, WI 53213
Email: info@halleonard.com

In Europe, contact:
Hal Leonard Europe Limited
1 Red Place
London, W1K 6PL
Email: info@halleonardeurope.com

In Australia, contact:
Hal Leonard Australia Pty. Ltd.
4 Lentara Court
Cheltenham, Victoria, 3192 Australia
Email: info@halleonard.com.au

Order No. AM27137

Book Design Phil Cleaver
Cover Design Phil Cleaver/Giuila Landor
Design Assistant Sue Tritton
Cover Photography John Stone
Illustration by 6 point Gill
Phototypesetting AGP Typesetting

Printed in the UK

Contents

Introduction The tin whistle is one of the nicest instruments you can learn to play. It is a simple instrument which is fun to play even in the early stages. It is particularly suited to the traditional music of England, Scotland, and Ireland, and many modern tunes can also be played on it.

You will be learning to play the whistle in the key of D. This is a very good one to learn as it can be played along with other instruments, such as the fiddle and the flute. It is easy to produce a good tone, and you do not have to spread your fingers as much as is necessary on some other whistles.

The whistle   Your tin whistle is a cylindrical metal tube with six holes, and a plastic mouthpiece at one end.
The sharp edge cut into the mouthpiece is called a fipple.

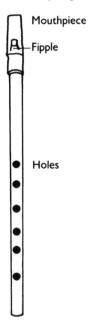

Mouthpiece

Fipple

Holes

What happens when   When you blow into the mouthpiece, the stream of air breaks
you blow   against the fipple and makes the column of air inside the tube vibrate. These vibrations create the sound.

Column of air flowing through whistle

Column of air is made to vibrate because of fipple

Vibrating column of air

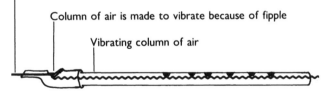

How to hold the whistle   Put the tip of the mouthpiece between your lips at the front of
your mouth without letting it touch your teeth.
Do not strain your lips; close them around the mouthpiece just
enough to direct the air into it.

Place your left thumb roughly beneath the first hole nearest the
mouthpiece to support the whistle.

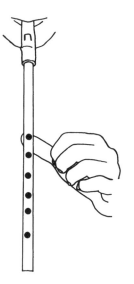

Covering the finger holes

Left hand   Place the pad of the first joint of the first finger of your left
hand over the first hole.

Then place the pad of the second finger of your left hand over
the second hole

and the pad of your third left finger over the third hole.

Your left little finger may be held loose below the tube where it
is probably most comfortable.

Right hand   Keep the first three holes covered with the first three fingers of
the left hand, and place your right thumb under the tube
beneath the fourth hole.

Now place the pad of the first finger of your right hand over
the fourth hole of the whistle.

Next place the pad of your second right hand finger over the
fifth hole

and then place the pad of your third right finger over the sixth
and last hole.

You will probably find it is easiest to hold your right little finger above the tube as you play.

Left hand

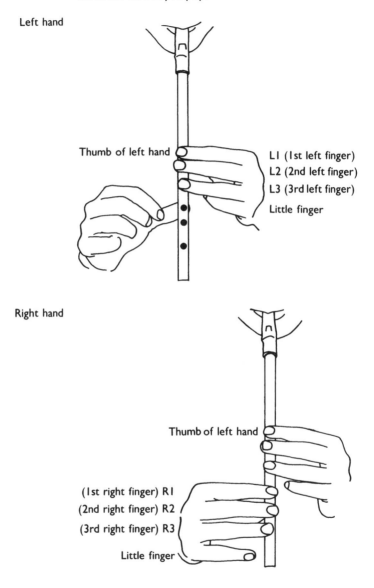

Thumb of left hand

LI (Ist left finger)
L2 (2nd left finger)
L3 (3rd left finger)

Little finger

Right hand

Thumb of left hand

(Ist right finger) RI
(2nd right finger) R2
(3rd right finger) R3

Little finger

Holding the whistle properly

Do not use the tips of your fingers to cover the holes - use the **pads** of your fingers.

Your fingers should be held **flat**, not curved over the tube. Do not grip hard.

Make sure the pads of your fingers are covering the holes **completely** — otherwise the notes you play will not be right and will not sound clear.

Left hand

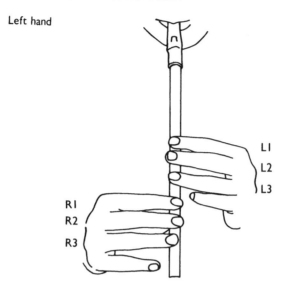

Always remember: The three holes closest to the mouthpiece are played with the first three fingers of the **LEFT** hand.

The three holes furthest from the mouthpiece are played with the first three fingers of the **RIGHT** hand.

You are now ready to play Keep holding the whistle as before, with all the holes covered completely with the pads of the correct fingers.

Blowing Now blow very gently. In fact, you need hardly do more than breathe through the mouthpiece.

The sound you have produced is the lowest sound which you can produce on your tin whistle.

Notes In music, sounds are represented by notes, which are named after the first seven letters of the alphabet.

You have just played the note **d.**

When written in musical notation it looks like this:

The head of the note is placed just below the lowest of five horizontal lines which are called the **stave**. The tail of the note sticks upwards from the head.

Now lift the third finger of your right hand off the 6th and last hole of the whistle and blow gently.

Right hand

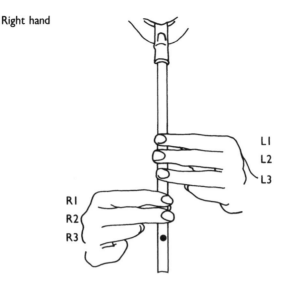

LI
L2
L3

RI
R2
R3

This sound is a tone higher than **d**. It is the note **e**.

When written in musical notation it looks like this:

The head of the note **e** is placed right on the bottom line of the stave.

e is the second note of the scale of D.

The scale   A scale is a progression of sounds, or notes, — with each one higher than the one before it.
A scale begins and ends on a note of the same name.

The scale of D begins on **d**, and ends on high **d**. It is very easy to play on the tin whistle.

How to play the scale of D   You begin by playing **d**, as you just learned, and then simply uncover each of the holes of your whistle, starting from the bottom up, to produce progressively higher sounds.

Now proceed to play the scale of D with the aid of the diagrams.

As you uncover each hole, remember to **blow gently**.

The fingering code is an easy way to remember the fingering for each note. Learn it as you go along.

o = open hole

● = covered hole

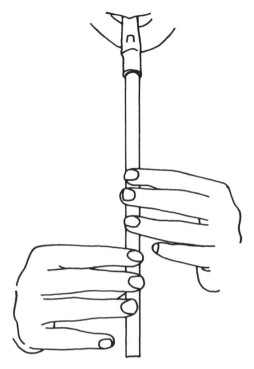

Note **d** To play the first note, keep all 6 holes well covered as they were before.

Diagram

Fingering Code **6**

Music Notation

Note **e** To play the next note keep the top 5 holes covered and lift your last finger, R3, off the bottom hole.

Diagram

Fingering Code **5**

Music Notation

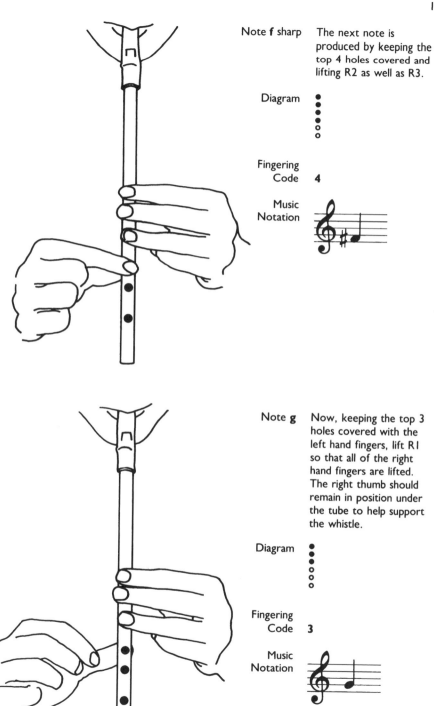

Note **f sharp** The next note is produced by keeping the top 4 holes covered and lifting R2 as well as R3.

Diagram

Fingering Code **4**

Music Notation

Note **g** Now, keeping the top 3 holes covered with the left hand fingers, lift R1 so that all of the right hand fingers are lifted. The right thumb should remain in position under the tube to help support the whistle.

Diagram

Fingering Code **3**

Music Notation

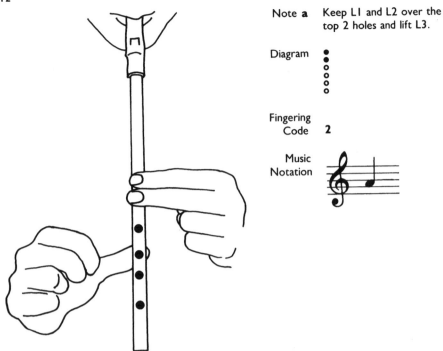

Note **a**   Keep L1 and L2 over the top 2 holes and lift L3.

Diagram

Fingering Code   **2**

Music Notation

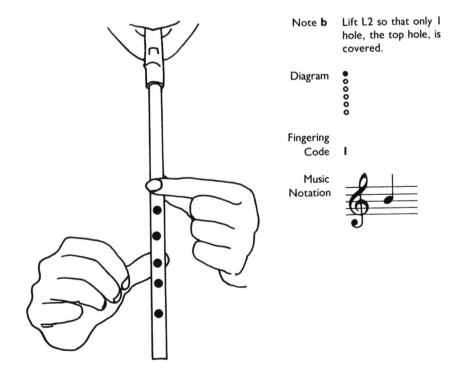

Note **b**   Lift L2 so that only 1 hole, the top hole, is covered.

Diagram

Fingering Code   **1**

Music Notation

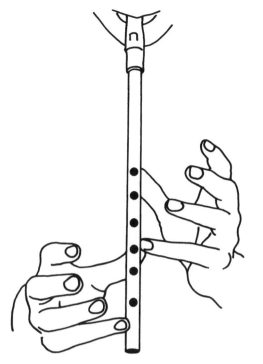

Note c sharp Now lift L1 as well. All the holes are now uncovered. You should be supporting the whistle with your right and left thumbs beneath the tube. If you place your little fingers on the sides of the tube this also helps to balance the whistle.

Diagram

Fingering Code **0**

Music Notation

Note high d Keep L1 lifted off the first hole, but cover the rest of the 5 holes with the correct fingers — L2, L3, R1, R2, R3. (You no longer need your little fingers for balance).

Diagram

Fingering Code **5**

Music Notation

Now play the the scale of D backwards, from high **d** to **d**.

Notice That the more holes you cover, the lower the sound is, and the fewer holes you cover, the higher the sound is, (except when you come to high **d**.)

Sharps The notes **f** and **c** in the scale of D are 'sharp'. A sharp raises a note a semitone, or half a tone. This means that a note which is sharp sounds slightly higher than it does when it is 'natural'.
f and **c** are always sharp in the scale of D in order to make the correct progression of sounds.

The symbol for sharp is ♯. It is placed on the stave just in front of the head of the note to which it refers.

The scale of D looks like this when written in musical notation:

Names of notes: **d**   **e**   **f**   **g**   **a**   **b**   **c**   **d**
                                     sharp   sharp   high

Treble clef sign The symbol at the beginning of the stave is a **treble clef** sign. It indicates that the notes following it on the stave will all be fairly high notes — such as those which can be produced on the tin whistle.

Notice that by convention the notes whose heads fall below the middle line of the stave have tails which point upwards, and the tails of notes whose heads are placed above the middle line point downwards.

The tail of **b** (on the middle line) can point either up or down.

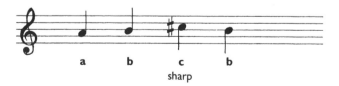

                a   **b**   **c**   **b**
                                     sharp

Tonguing Before you play the scale of D again, learn the 'tonguing' technique. This enables you to produce a clean start and end to each note: first put your tongue up against the roof of your mouth. Then when you blow out, drop your tongue quickly at the same time; that is, sound a soft letter 't', ie say 'tuh', — or to put it another way, spit gently.

To end the note cleanly, put your tongue back up against the roof of your mouth to cut off the flow of your breath.

Now 'tongue' each note of the scale of D.
As you play, try to follow the notes written on the stave instead of looking at the diagrams!

Baa Baa Black Sheep

Note values   You have learned enough notes to play your first tune on the tin whistle. But before you do so, study the different note values below so that you will know how long to hold each note in the tune.

This type of note, which we used to write the scale of D in musical notation, is a **crotchet**. A crotchet is worth one count.

The first four notes of Baa Baa Black Sheep are each held for one count.

A crotchet with a flag on its tail is called a **quaver**. A quaver is held only half as long (and therefore played twice as fast) as a crotchet, so it is worth only half of a count.

The next four notes of Baa Baa Black Sheep are played twice as fast as the first four so quavers are used. When there are two or more quavers together in a tune their flags are usually straightened and joined together as shown here.

A **minim** is held for twice as long as a crotchet and is worth two counts.

So is the next note in Baa Baa Black Sheep.

Baa Baa Black Sheep is written out below in musical notation.

The beat   Sing the song out loud before you play it, and as you sing clap out a steady beat as shown, by clapping once for each crotchet, or whole count.
So — there will be 2 quavers to each steady clap, and two claps for each minim.

Baa Baa Black Sheep

Now play the tune on your tin whistle. The fingering codes and diagrams have been included to help you.

You may want to tap out the steady beat with your foot as you play.

Breathing   When you come to this sign ♪ take a breath!

Practising   In order to play any tune fluently, practise each **phrase** (i.e. the notes you play in one breath), and any group of notes which gives you trouble until you perfect them. Then play the tune from start to finish.

Tonguing this tune　When you can play Baa Baa Black Sheep smoothly try using the tonguing technique:

Tongue all the crotchets and minims, but only the first quaver in each group of quavers.

Always make sure you drop your tongue both quickly and softly or you will not produce clean notes.

Frère Jacques

Now try the second song. You probably know it well. Hum it and clap out the steady beat as shown before you play it on your whistle.

This time do not tongue the notes.

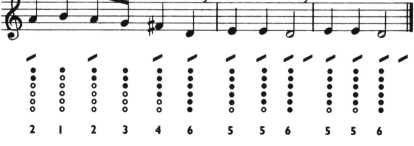

More notes   Blowing harder

Play the note **e** as you were taught — blowing very gently.

blow gently   ●
    e   ●
       ●
       ●
       ○
       5

Now, without changing your fingering, blow a little bit harder through the mouthpiece, — but not too hard or your instrument will screech!

blow harder   ●
  high **e**   ●
       ●
       ●
       ○
       5

The note you have played is high **e**.

Next, lift R2 to play **f♯** blowing gently.

blow gently   ●   Now blow a bit harder.   ●
   f♯   ●   high **f♯**   ●
      ●   ●
      ○   ○
      ○   ○
      4   **4**

The note you have played is high **f♯**.

Repeat this process for the notes **g**, **a**, **b**, **c♯** and high **d**:
First play each note as you learned before when you played the scale of D,—blowing gently.

Then play the same note again,—blowing a bit harder.

blow gently   ●   blow gently   ●   blow gently   ●
   g   ●   **a**   ○   **b**   ○
      ○   ○   ○
blow harder   ○   blow harder   ○   blow harder   ○
  high **g**   ○   high **a**   ○   high **b**   ○
      3   **2**   **1**

blow gently   ○   blow gently   ○
   c♯   ○   **d**   ●
      ○   ●
blow harder   ○   blow harder   ●
  high **c♯**   ○   high **d**   ●
      0   **0**
                        5

Each time you blew harder in this exercise, you played each note an octave higher than when you blew gently.

The octave   One octave is 8 notes.
The first octave of the scale of D consists of the first 8 notes
you learned — from **d** to high **d**.

The second octave of the scale of D consists of each of these
same 8 notes played one octave higher, by simply blowing harder
on your whistle — as you have just done!

Notice: (Since high **d** is one octave higher than **d**, you can in fact play it
by using the fingering for **d (6)** and blowing harder. But the
sound you produce using that method is less clear than if you lift
L1 and play it the way you first learned.)

Leger lines   **The second octave of the scale of D** is written out in musical
notation below.

Notice   The higher notes simply continue higher up on the stave, from
where the first octave left off.

But as there are not enough lines of a stave to accommodate all
the notes of the second octave, extra lines, called **leger lines**,
must be added for the last four notes.

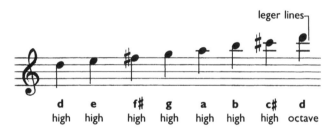

	d	e	f♯	g	a	b	c♯	d
	high	high	high	high	high	high	high	octave

Play the second octave, following the musical notation.

Remember do not blow **too** hard to begin with. But you will
find that you have to blow increasingly harder to produce the
highest notes.

Tonguing the second octave   When you are able to play each note with a good clear sound,
try using the tonguing technique for each note. You will find
that you have to tongue a bit more sharply than you did for the
first octave in order to produce clear notes.

The first and second octaves of the scale of D are written out
together below.

The second octave notes' names and code numbers underlined
in italics — and will be from now on — to distinguish them from
the notes in the first octave.

Octave **d** is written **_d_**.

Key signature

Key signature

Notice that on the stave after the treble clef sign there are two sharp signs — one placed on the line belonging to f, and the other on the space belonging to **c**.

These two sharp signs make up the key signature of the key of D. When a tune is in the key of D, this key signature tells you that all the **f**'s and **c**'s, high and low, which occur in that tune are to be played sharp — as you've learned them, — so it is not necessary to place a sharp sign before every **f** and **c** in the tune.

Play both octaves, one after the other, taking a breath after high **d** and tonguing each note.

Remembering the names of notes

It is easy to remember the names of the notes on the stave: The notes placed on the lines can be remembered as being the first letters of the words in the saying: **e**very **g**ood **b**oy **d**eserves **f**avour.

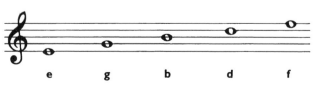

The notes on the spaces between the lines spell **face**.

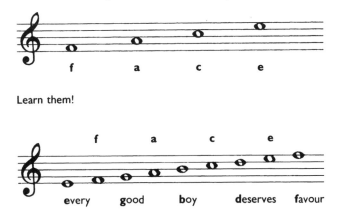

Learn them!

Skip To My Lou

This tune uses notes mainly from the second octave of the D scale, so remember that for the most part you must blow harder than you did to play the notes of the first two songs you learned.

But have a close look at the musical notation before you play it:

Notice that the key signature of the key of D has been included, and that there are three new things indicated for you to learn:

Bar lines Divide the music into equal bars, or measures. Each bar in any one tune contains the same number of beats as the other bars in the tune.

Time signature Tells you how many beats there will be in each bar, and also the value of the beats. As you can see, the time signature consists of two numbers, placed one beneath the other after the key signature on the stave. Skip to my Lou is in 4/4 single time.

The top 4 tells you that there are 4 beats in each bar.
The bottom 4 means that one crotchet counts for one beat.

The 4 beats in each bar have been counted out for you here.

A double bar line Indicates the end of the piece.

Practise this tune phrase by phrase first, and tap out the steady beat — one tap for each crotchet value, or each whole count.

You should tongue all the notes in this tune except the second quaver in the penultimate bar.

Skip to my Lou

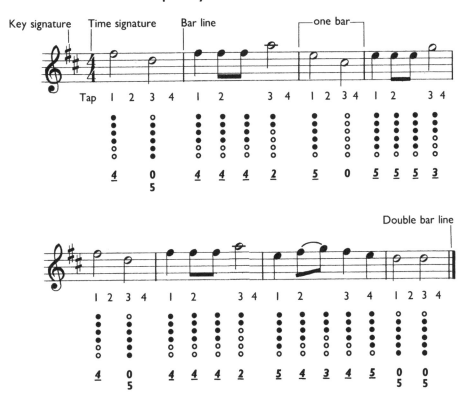

Tonguing in general   As a general rule only the first of a group of quavers or semiquavers should be tongued. But tonguing is really a matter for you to decide once you have the feel of a tune. Therefore, except in special cases we will give very few tonguing instructions from now on.

Yankee Doodle

The next song uses notes from both octaves, so only blow harder on the notes above high **d**.

It is also in 4/4 time — 4 crotchet beats in each bar.

Practise it phrase by phrase, and tap out the beat as you did with the previous tunes.

23

Yankee Doodle

Shepherd's Hey

Before you proceed to learn different time signatures, practise this next tune in 4/4 time bar by bar to develop your finger agility. It is an English Country Dance tune.

Notice something new The double bar line with two dots in front of it means 'repeat'. When you come to this sign you must repeat the section you just played from the beginning, or from the previous backwards repeat sign if there is one.

So in this piece you must play the first four bars twice, then the next four bars twice, and then the last four bars twice!

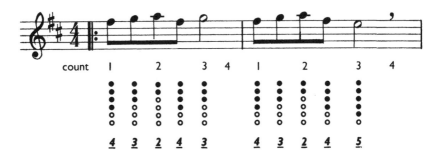

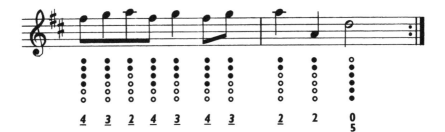

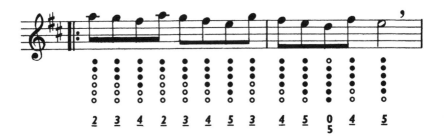

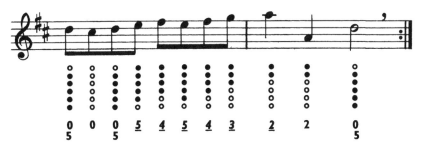

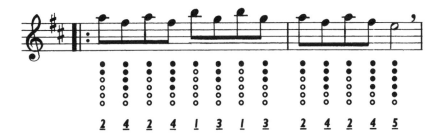

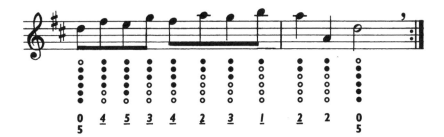

More time signatures

In all time signatures:
The **top** number tells you how many beats there are in each bar and the **bottom** number tells you the value of the beats.

So far you have only encountered crotchet beats.
You know that if the bottom number is 4, a **crotchet** counts for one beat.

But, if the bottom number is 8, a **quaver** counts for one beat.

Here is a list of most of the time signatures you will come across:

4 crotchet-beats to a bar

count 1   2   3   4

So all the notes in one bar add up to 4 crotchets.

also known as
Common Time

1   2   3   4

And written C.

3 crotchet-beats to a bar

1   2   3

So all the notes in one bar add up to 3 crotchets.

2 crotchet-beats to a bar

1   2

So all the notes in one bar add up to 2 crotchets.

6 quaver-beats to a bar

1   2   3   4   5   6

So all the notes in one bar add up to 6 quavers.

9 quaver-beats to a bar

1   2   3   4   5   6   7   8   9

So all the notes in one bar add up to 9 quavers.

12 quaver-beats to a bar

1   2   3   4   5   6   7   8   9   10   11   12

So all the notes in one bar add up to 12 quavers.

No matter what sort of beat a tune may have, a quaver is always to be played twice as quickly as a crotchet (or held half

as long), and a minim will always be played twice as slowly as a
crotchet (or held twice as long).

A Visit to Ireland
Here is a tune in 6/8 time — 6 quaver-beats to a bar — that is,
a quaver counts as 1 beat and there are 6 quavers to a bar.
The beats are counted out to help you.

Notice   That this tune begins on the last beat of a bar. Any tune (or any
section in it) that begins with an incomplete bar will also end in
an incomplete bar, but the two together will add up to the
correct number of beats for one bar.

The Ashgrove

Now try this lovely Welsh song in 3/4 time.
The first few bars are counted out for you.

2 2 0 5 4 2 3 4 0 5 0 5

5 3 4 5 0 5 0 2 2 0 5 4 5 0 5 0

1 3 1 2 0 5 0 0 5

More note values

 An open oval shaped note is a **semibreve**. It is held for four counts, — four times as long as a crotchet.

A quaver with a second flag added on is called a **semiquaver**. It is played twice as fast as a quaver, so it is only held for ¼ of a count.

 When there is a group of 2 or more semiquavers together, they are joined together in the same manner as quavers.

The table on the next page shows clearly all of the note values you have learned so far and how they relate to each other.

Notice   that the crotchet is used as the standard, and for convenience we give it a value of one count, and relate the other note values to it.

But remember — it only counts as one beat in a tune if the bottom number of the time signature is 4.

Table of note values
semibreve

minim

crotchet

quaver

semiquaver

4 counts

2 counts

1 count

½ count

¼ count

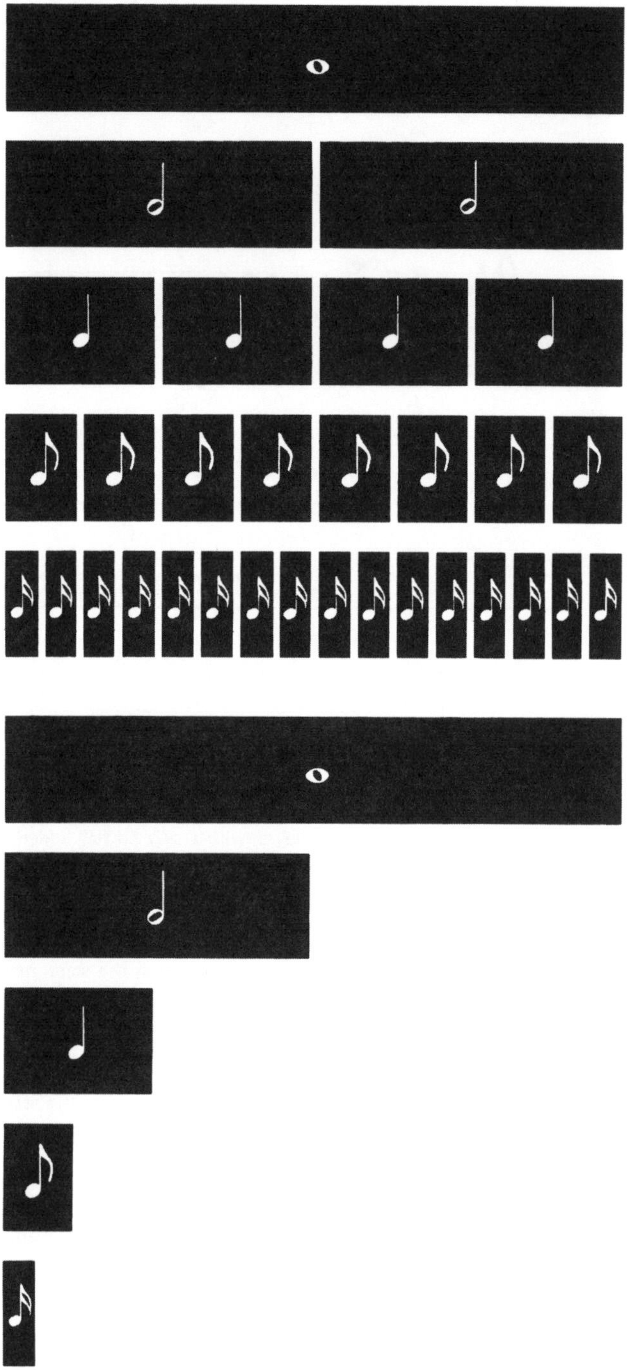

The Drunken Sailor

This song has semiquavers for you to try. It is a brisk tune which no doubt you know well.

Tonguing fast repeated notes

tuh tuh kuh

When you come to the pairs of semiquavers try a slightly different tonguing action from the one you learned before, — as if to say 'tuh kuh':

This helps you to play the semiquavers up to speed. Pairs of quavers or semiquavers of the same note should usually be tongued in this manner.

Counting half beats

On fast tunes such as this one it may help you to count the half beats — by saying 'and'.

Dotted notes   If a note has a dot right after it, that means you must hold the note for its own total time value plus half of its own time value.

dotted minim
2 + 1 = 3 counts

dotted crotchet
1 + ½ = 1½ counts

dotted quaver
½ + ¼ = ¾ of a count

Complete table of note values

4 counts	
3 counts	
2 counts	
1½ counts	
1 count	
¾ of a count	
½ of a count	
⅜ of a count	
¼ of a count	

God Save The Queen

This is a tune with dotted crotchets and a dotted minim.

Oranges and Lemons

Here is a song with a dotted minim in it.

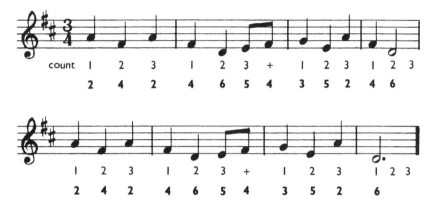

Plaisir D'Amour (The Joys of Love)

The next song is a beautiful, slow love song. It has tied notes in it.

The tie   A tie is a curved line which joins two or more of the SAME note together. You are to play only the first note of a tie and hold it unbroken without repeating it for the total time value of the two (or more) notes in the tie.

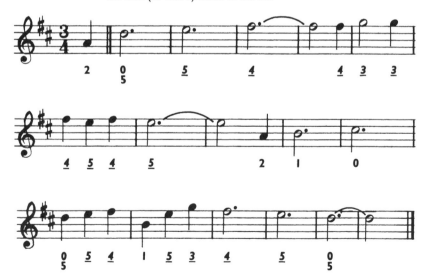

Rests   Sometimes in the middle of a tune there are points at which no note is played. These points are called rests.
Like notes, rests are held for different lengths of time, and there are different symbols to show how long the silence should last.

Table of rests

semibreve rest
4 counts

minim rest
2 counts

crotchet rest
1 count

quaver rest
½ a count

semiquaver rest
¼ of a count

Good Night Ladies

This tune has crotchet rests as well as tied notes.

The scale of G   So far you have only played tunes in the key of D. But you can also play tunes in the key of G on your whistle.

(You can play only one complete octave of the G scale because octave **d** is the highest note the tin whistle can produce clearly.)

The scale of G begins on **g** and ends on high **g**.
And there is only one sharp note in the scale of G — **f♯**.

Therefore, there is only one sharp in the key signature of G.

c natural   When you come to **c**, you play **c** natural instead of **c** sharp.

The sign for 'natural' is ♮.

The most common method of playing **c** natural is this way:

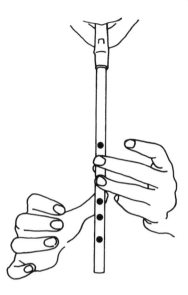

Now play the scale of G and tongue each note.

g	a	b	c	d	e	f♯	g
3	2	1	0	0	5	4	3
			2	5			

Hearing the difference

Remember that a sharp raises a note a semitone.
Can you hear the difference between a whole tone and a semitone? ...

Play c♮, then play c♯.
c♯ is a **semitone** higher than c♮.

Play c♮ again. Then play high **d**.
High **d** is a **whole tone** higher than c♮.

always check the key signature of a piece before you begin to play it!

38

Minuet in G by Bach

Triplets   A triplet consists of 3 notes played in the time of 2.

minim triplets
are played to the time
value of:

2 minims

or one semibreve.

crotchet triplets
are played to the time
value of:

two crotchets

or one minim.

quaver triplets
are played to the time
value of:

two quavers

or one crotchet.

semiquaver triplets
are played to the time
value of:

two semiquavers

or one quaver.

Tonguing triplets When tonguing triplets of either quavers or semiquavers you will probably find it is easiest to tongue them 'tuh kuh tuh'.

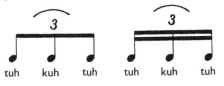

tuh   kuh   tuh   tuh   kuh   tuh

Amazing Grace

Here is a tune with quaver triplets — the first few bars are counted out for you.

Taking care of your whistle Your tin whistle might get clogged with spit after some time. If you cannot blow it clear (by blowing forcefully through the mouthpiece) you should clean it out with a pipe cleaner.

If the pitch of your whistle becomes sharp — too high — you can bring it down to the right pitch by loosening the mouthpiece a bit. If you find it difficult to twist the mouthpiece put the whistle in hot — but not boiling — water and try again.